STEM

IN OUR WORLD

MOVIEMAKING TECHNOLOGY:
4D, MOTION CAPTURE, AND MORE

BY JOHN WOOD

©2018
Book Life
King's Lynn
Norfolk PE30 4LS

ISBN: 978-1-78637-298-7

All rights reserved
Printed in Malaysia

Written by:
John Wood

Edited by:
Holly Duhig

Designed by:
Daniel Scase

A catalogue record for this book
is available from the British Library.

STEM
IN OUR WORLD

PRODUCTION

DIRECTOR

SCENE | TAKE | ROLL

DATE

ADMIT ONE
66929

CONTENTS

WORDS THAT LOOK LIKE *THIS* ARE EXPLAINED
IN THE GLOSSARY ON PAGE 31.

WELCOME TO STEM SCHOOL

ATTENTION, STUDENTS. MY NAME IS PROFESSOR TESS TUBE, AND I AM YOUR TEACHER. BY READING THIS BOOK, YOU ARE NOW PART OF STEM SCHOOL. STEM STANDS FOR:

SCIENCE, TECHNOLOGY, ENGINEERING AND MATHS.

OH, I'VE JUST GOT A MESSAGE. IT SEEMS THAT SOME PEOPLE ARE COMING TO MAKE A MOVIE ABOUT OUR SCHOOL – AND THEY WANT TO INTERVIEW ME! THEY'LL BE HERE ANY MINUTE. B–BUT I'VE NEVER DONE AN INTERVIEW BEFORE. WHAT WILL I DO? WHAT WILL I SAY? I HAVE TO FIND SOMEWHERE TO HIDE...

BUT STEM ISN'T ALL ABOUT BEING FAMOUS. STEM IS IMPORTANT IN ALL SORTS OF WAYS.

WHY IS STEM IMPORTANT IN ALL SORTS OF WAYS?

You can probably find STEM in almost every part of your life. Here are a few examples:

- COMPUTERS AT SCHOOL, WHICH HELP US LEARN
- TOASTERS, KETTLES AND OVENS AT HOME, WHICH HELP US MAKE FOOD AND DRINK
- HOSPITAL MACHINES AND MEDICINE, WHICH HELP US LIVE LONGER
- CARS, BOATS AND PLANES, WHICH HELP US TRAVEL AROUND THE WORLD QUICKLY
- WEATHER REPORTS THAT TELL US WHAT THE WEATHER IS GOING TO BE LIKE

STEM is all about understanding and solving problems in the real world. When we have an idea of how something might work, we test it again and again to make sure it is right. Then we can create machines and **SYSTEMS** to solve the problems we have.

Sometimes we get new information, and find out that our old ideas were wrong. But that is OK – STEM subjects are all about changing your ideas based on the information you have.

I DON'T KNOW IF YOU REALISE, CHILDREN, BUT THE IDEA OF BEING IN A MOVIE MAKES ME A LITTLE BIT SCARED! OK, LET'S SEE WHAT YOU ARE GOING TO LEARN ABOUT TODAY. TALKING ABOUT STEM ALWAYS CALMS ME DOWN...

STEM IN MOVIES

HOW MANY MOVIES ARE MADE?

Every year, over 500 movies are made in **HOLLYWOOD**. When you walk into the cinema, you might be seeing a movie about space, or dinosaurs, or superheroes – anything can happen on the movie screen.

HOLLYWOOD IS THE OLDEST **FILM INDUSTRY** IN THE WORLD, AND MAKES THE MOST MONEY.

BOLLYWOOD, IN INDIA, IS ALSO AN IMPORTANT FILM INDUSTRY. IT MAKES OVER 1,000 MOVIES EVERY YEAR, MORE THAN ANY OTHER FILM INDUSTRY.

IMPORTANT INVENTIONS AND IDEAS IN MOVIES

In 1877, Eadweard Muybridge wanted to see exactly how horses run. He built a course with 12 cameras that each took a picture as the horse ran past. Using a lantern and a **ROTATING** disc, Muybridge quickly shone each photo onto a screen, one after the other. This made it seem like the picture was moving.

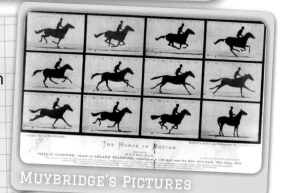

MUYBRIDGE'S PICTURES

In 1895, two brothers called Auguste and Louis Lumière built the cinématographe, which was a cross between a camera and a **PROJECTOR**. It was a very popular machine because it was light and powered by turning a handle.

THE CINÉMATOGRAPHE WAS PROBABLY THE MOST IMPORTANT EARLY MOTION PICTURE CAMERA.

Georges Méliès, a French magician, began making movies around 1896. His movies were different to what had already been done because he used camera tricks and special effects. He made movies which had lots of different **SCENES** that told a story.

THIS IS A SCENE FROM A TRIP TO THE MOON, MADE BY GEORGES MÉLIÈS IN 1902.

Technology has made **FILMING** cheaper and easier, which means that bigger, more exciting movies can be made. Technology has also made special effects and camera tricks much more realistic. Sometimes it can be hard to tell what is real and what isn't when watching a movie.

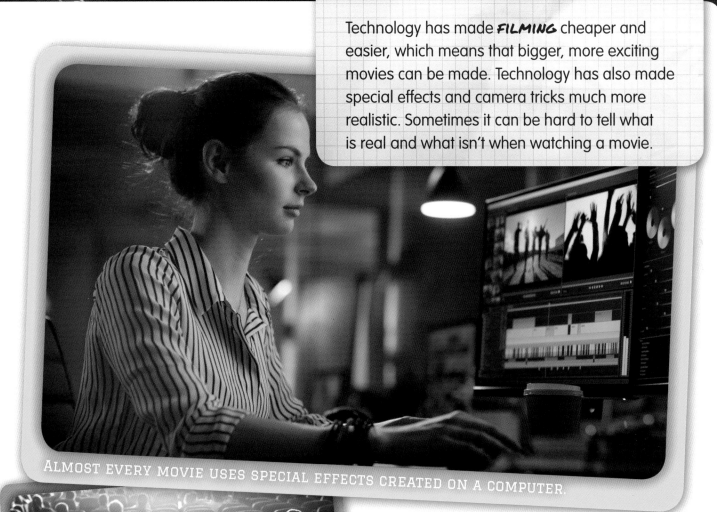

ALMOST EVERY MOVIE USES SPECIAL EFFECTS CREATED ON A COMPUTER.

Movies are important. They tell us stories about good people vs bad people. They tell us about the past and show us what the future might be like. We need to do STEM research into movies, so we can keep telling stories in new and interesting ways.

BRRRRRRRIIII NNNNNGGGGG!

AH, THE BELL! LIGHTS! CAMERA! SCIENCE! REMEMBER, IF YOU SEE ANYONE TRYING TO FILM ME, BE SURE TO LET ME KNOW! I NEED TO DO WHATEVER IT TAKES TO GET OUT OF THIS INTERVIEW. LET'S TURN THE PAGE AND SEE WHAT WE'RE GOING TO LEARN ABOUT FIRST...

ANIMATRONICS

MECHANICAL MONSTERS

Animatronics are **MECHANICAL** machines that are mostly used in movies to create characters and creatures which don't exist in the real world, such as dinosaurs, aliens or giant robots. Today, movies would usually use **CGI** to create these things. However, sometimes CGI is not realistic enough, especially if something is going to be filmed close-up. In this case, animatronics might be used instead. This happened a lot more in the 1980s and 1990s, but there are still some movies using animatronics today.

ANIMATRONICS ARE USEFUL FOR **ACTORS** BECAUSE EVERYONE CAN SEE WHAT THE CREATURE OR CHARACTER WILL LOOK LIKE WHEN FILMING.

JURASSIC PARK TO JURASSIC WORLD

AN ANIMATRONIC TYRANNOSAURUS REX

In 1993, a movie called Jurassic Park was made, which was all about dinosaurs. To create the dinosaurs, movie-makers used animatronics. Their Tyrannosaurus rex was the biggest animatronic creature ever made at the time. Although Jurassic World mostly used CGI for the dinosaurs in 2015, an animatronic dinosaur was also created for some close-up moments.

ANIMATRONICS ARE ALSO USED ALL OVER THE WORLD IN THEME PARKS.

I'VE GOT IT! IF ANYBODY COMES ROUND TO FILM ME, I'LL SET THESE ANIMATRONICS INTO KILL MODE! HUH, THAT'S WEIRD... THERE DOESN'T SEEM TO BE A KILL MODE. WHAT KIND OF STRANGE SCIENTIST CREATED THESE ROBOTS? HONESTLY.

To move all the different parts, most simple animatronics use something called a servomotor, or servo for short. Here are some things that make up a servomotor:

A motor is a device which turns electricity into movement. Inside a motor, metal parts rotate. The amount it spins is called its torque.

SENSOR

Servos have sensors inside which know exactly how much the motor needs to turn to make something move. This makes servos very good at small, accurate movements, which are the kind of movements animatronics make.

GEARS

The rotating parts of a motor can be attached to a gear. A gear is a wheel with teeth which can be fitted together with other gears of different sizes. When little gears are fitted into bigger gears, the little motor can move much bigger objects.

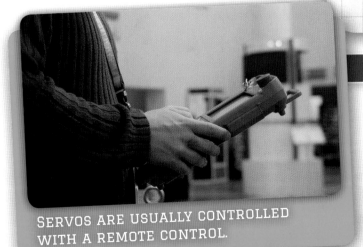

SERVOS ARE USUALLY CONTROLLED WITH A REMOTE CONTROL.

HOW DO ANIMATRONICS MOVE?

Strings, rods and **PADDLES** connect the servos to the parts of an animatronic that move, like arms, eyebrows or mouths. When the motor spins, the strings, rods and paddles move. In complicated animatronics, servos control little things, like making a dinosaur blink.

3D MOVIES

2D AND 3D

In 3D movies, some objects seem far away and some seem so close that you could touch them. However, most movies are 2D. 2D objects have a height (up and down) and a width (side to side). If you put your finger on this page, you can move your finger up and down or side to side. That means everything on this page is 2D.

Most objects in the world are 3D. A 3D object has a height (up and down), a width (side to side) and a depth (forwards and backwards). In 3D movies things can go up and down, side to side, and also closer and farther away.

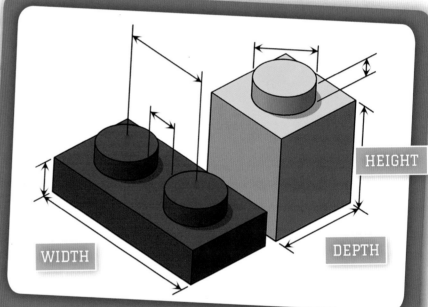

HEIGHT

WIDTH

DEPTH

CAN YOU TELL WHICH APPLE IS 3D?

If you look through one eye at a time, you will see that each eye sees a slightly different **IMAGE**. When you look at an object with both eyes open, your brain mixes the two separate images from each eye and creates the 3D image. This is how we see the world in 3D.

3D movies project two images at once from the same screen. This looks strange and blurry until the viewer puts on special 3D glasses. The glasses separate the two images, so your left eye sees one image and your right eye sees the other. This allows your brain to mix them together and create a 3D image, just like it does with everyday objects.

NO MORE 3D GLASSES

Some TVs and cinemas are using technology which creates 3D without the need for glasses. These special screens have a barrier inside with slits all along it. The slits break up the two images projected by the screen, and a different one is sent to each eye. Your brain then mixes the images together.

3D CINEMA

UNLIKE MOST CINEMA SCREENS, MIT'S 3D CINEMA IS VERY SMALL AT THE MOMENT, SO THIS TECHNOLOGY ISN'T READY FOR EVERYONE JUST YET.

Massachusetts Institute of Technology (MIT) and the Weizmann Institute of Science have invented a **PROTOTYPE** for a 3D cinema screen that doesn't need glasses. The screen uses mirrors to reflect the light all around the cinema in clever ways. This means the different images will be sent to each of the eyes no matter where the viewer sits.

4D

A 4D movie uses more than sound and screen to show a movie. All sorts of special effects are used, from seats that rock back and forth to water splashed on the viewers. There are around 150 cinemas in the world that use 4D effects. Some people think this will be the future of movies, because it is an experience that you cannot get at home.

FLASHING LIGHTS!

WATER SPRAYED ON YOUR CLOTHES!

AIR BLOWING IN YOUR FACE!

A PUNCH IN THE BACK!

MIST AND FOG!

GOOD SMELLS!

BAD SMELLS!

OVER 30 COUNTRIES ALL OVER THE WORLD HAVE A 4D CINEMA.

HAS SCIENCE GONE TOO FAR?

Everything that happens to the viewers while watching a 4D movie is part of the story happening on screen. So, if there is a chase, the seats would move. Water would be splashed on the audience if the character fell in a river or crossed a stream. This is meant to make the story feel even more real, as if you are there alongside the main character.

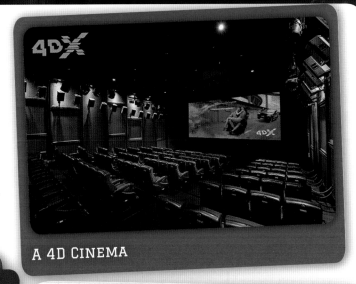

A 4D CINEMA

4D CINEMA WAS INVENTED IN SOUTH KOREA IN 2009.

Although 4D cinemas are becoming more popular, there aren't many of them compared to normal cinemas. If a cinema has 4D effects, there are usually special seats that the viewer must sit in. There are more 4D cinemas in some Asian countries, such as South Korea. However, not everybody thinks they are a good idea. Some people think that 4D is a bad idea and don't want to be shaken around while they are trying to eat their popcorn. What do you think? Would you try it?

DO YOU THINK 4D IS THE FUTURE OF MOVIES?

GREEN SCREEN

Movies are full of impossible, magical things. In the cinema we see superheroes flying around, dragons breathing fire and alien planets looming in the distance. To create these impossible things, movies use a type of special effect called CGI. However, inserting CGI into a scene can be difficult. To make it easier, technology called chroma keying is used. It also goes by a different name – green screen.

GREEN SCREEN

WHAT IS CHROMA KEYING?

A MOVIE STUDIO CAN HAVE ACTORS AND REAL OBJECTS ALONGSIDE THE GREEN SCREENS. THE CGI IS ADDED TO THE MOVIE LATER.

Chroma keying is used to insert CGI or other special effects into a scene. It works by removing a single shade of colour from an image and replacing it with something else. Movie-makers usually use screens that are a bright shade of green when they film a scene. This is why it is sometimes known as green screen.

Chroma keying is done using a video *EDITING* program on a computer. When editing the video, the editor tells the computer to replace everything green with something else, like a CGI character or a different background.

A TYPE OF CHROMA KEYING WAS INVENTED IN THE 1930s, ALTHOUGH IT DIDN'T INVOLVE COMPUTERS. NOWADAYS, ALMOST EVERY BIG MOVIE YOU SEE AT THE CINEMA HAS PROBABLY USED CHROMA KEYING AT SOME POINT.

GREEN SCREEN AS A BACKGROUND

If a movie-maker wants a superhero to look like they are flying through the sky, the actor would be filmed lying down or hanging on wires in front of a big green screen. Using chroma keying, the colour green would then be removed from the scene and replaced with a video of the sky whizzing past. However, it is important that nobody else is wearing any green, otherwise that will also disappear and be replaced by the computer.

SUITS AND PROPS

THE GREEN SCREEN IN THE MOVIE HAS BEEN REPLACED WITH SPECIAL EFFECTS.

SOMETIMES BLUE SCREENS ARE USED INSTEAD OF GREEN SCREENS.

Chroma keying isn't just used to change the background. Parts of a costume or a prop might be green, or covered in a green fabric. This would make it possible to change the colour, or add any other effect to that object.

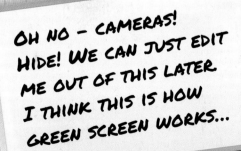

OH NO – CAMERAS! HIDE! WE CAN JUST EDIT ME OUT OF THIS LATER I THINK THIS IS HOW GREEN SCREEN WORKS...

MOTION CAPTURE

Motion capture is a piece of technology which can track how a person or object is moving in the real world. This movement can be copied by a CGI character or object. This makes the CGI movement more realistic and easier to make. Sometimes motion capture is used in scenes with other actors. This is helpful for the actors because it gives them a real person to act with.

A MOTION CAPTURE STUDIO

HOW DOES MOTION CAPTURE WORK?

Motion capture uses tiny markers that are placed all over the body. These markers are made of retroreflective material, which means that they only reflect light back in the direction of the light source.

THESE MARKERS WILL CAPTURE MOVEMENT ON THE FACE.

THE MARKERS ARE PLACED ALL OVER THE BODY, AND ON ANY PROPS.

Special cameras are placed around the studio. These cameras send constant flashes of light. Usually, this is a special type of light called infrared, which has less energy. Infrared light is invisible to humans, but the cameras can see it perfectly. The infrared light is reflected back by the markers and the cameras record where the markers are as they move around the studio.

The information picked up by the cameras is then sent to a computer. In a special program, the computer keeps a record of where the markers went and how they moved. The markers are then mapped onto the CGI character. So, for example, the CGI character's hand will follow the marker that was attached to the human's hand. The CGI character can now follow the human's movements exactly.

THIS IS THE VOICE OF YOUR TEACHER, TESS! THOSE CAMERAS WILL NEVER CATCH ME NOW, I'VE GOT MY STEALTH SUIT ON. WAIT, YOU CAN SEE MY GLASSES? FIDDLESTICKS - WHERE DID MY STEALTH GOGGLES GO?

FAMOUS MOTION CAPTURE ACTORS

One of the most famous motion capture actors is Andy Serkis. He has created the movements and facial expressions of many CGI characters such as Gollum in The Lord of the Rings, King Kong, and Caesar in The Planet of the Apes.

Sometimes it is just the actor's face that is tracked by motion capture. For example, actor Benedict Cumberbatch played a dragon in The Hobbit. The dragon's face followed Cumberbatch's facial movements, but its body was *ANIMATED* by CGI.

ANDY SERKIS

BENEDICT CUMBERBATCH PLAYED SMAUG THE DRAGON.

17

DRONES

A drone is an aircraft without a pilot which is sometimes remote-controlled. However, unlike a remote-control helicopter or aeroplane, a drone is able to control parts of its own flight. Today's drones are often fitted with cameras to perform all sorts of jobs, such as surveying dangerous areas, tracking wildlife and recording famous events. Moviemakers have also used camera drones to get especially difficult and interesting *SHOTS*.

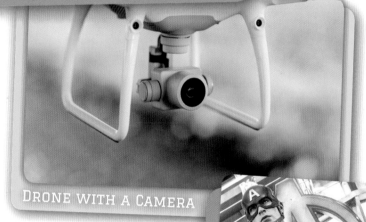

DRONE WITH A CAMERA

THE ONLY SHOTS THESE CAMERA DRONES ARE GOING TO GET ARE FROM MY LASER GUN.

CAPTAIN AMERICA

MOVIES THAT HAVE USED DRONES

Captain America: Civil War, which was filmed in 2015, used drones when filming in an airport. The airport scene was very complicated, with lots of fighting and special effects. The drones were used to film big, overhead shots.

In 2012, Skyfall also used a drone to film a scene in Istanbul. In the scene, James Bond uses a motorbike to chase a man across some rooftops. Filming the chase from the sky and keeping up with the motorbikes would have been very difficult without drone technology.

Sensors give the drone information about the world around it. Sensors help a drone figure out where it needs to go, and can even help the drone push against the wind so it is not blown off course. The ability to control itself is what makes a drone so stable. A stable drone is good for filming because it means the camera isn't shaky and the pictures aren't blurry.

THE DRONE CAN BE CONTROLLED WITH A REMOTE CONTROL THAT USES RADIO WAVES TO TELL THE DRONE WHAT TO DO.

HOW DO DRONES FLY?

Drones fly using **ROTORS**, which are powered by electricity. Drones can have around four to eight rotors. The rotors push air downwards, which sends the drone upwards. When a drone wants to change direction, it tilts itself so the rotors are pushing the air to one side, sending the drone in the opposite direction.

The drone has a battery which keeps the rotors spinning. However, the drone needs to be light so it can easily fly. This means a small, light battery must be used, which cannot power the drone for very long.

MOST DRONES CAN ONLY FLY FOR AROUND 12-25 MINUTES.

3D PRINTING

MAKING A MOVIE CAN BE HARD WORK, ESPECIALLY WHEN YOU THINK OF ALL THE STUFF THAT HAS TO BE MADE! A MOVIE SET IS FULL OF ALL SORTS OF THINGS, FROM SUPERHERO HAMMERS TO LIGHTSABERS – LUCKY FOR US, TECHNOLOGY CALLED 3D PRINTING HAS BEEN INVENTED.

BUILDING FROM THE GROUND UP

THIS IS A SMALL 3D PRINTER THAT MIGHT BE USED IN A HOME.

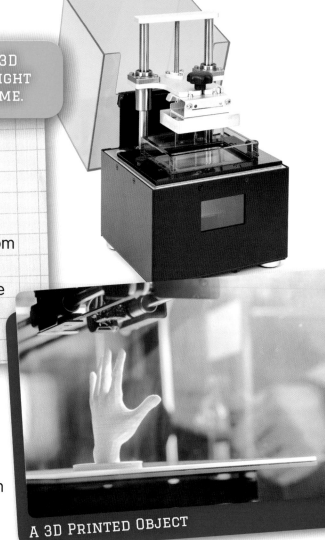

3D printing allows us to create and print out almost any type of object we want, all from one machine. All that is needed to create the object is a 3D printer, a design for the object and the right material to print with. At the moment the objects are mostly made from plastics, metals, glass, and sometimes chocolate, although in the future we may 3D-print objects made out of all sorts of materials, even living *TISSUE*.

For movies, 3D printing could be used to create props and sets that do not exist in the real world. For example, an army of aliens would need a lot of strange weapons that can't be bought in a shop. However, 3D printing allows movie-makers to design and print as many objects as they need.

A 3D PRINTED OBJECT

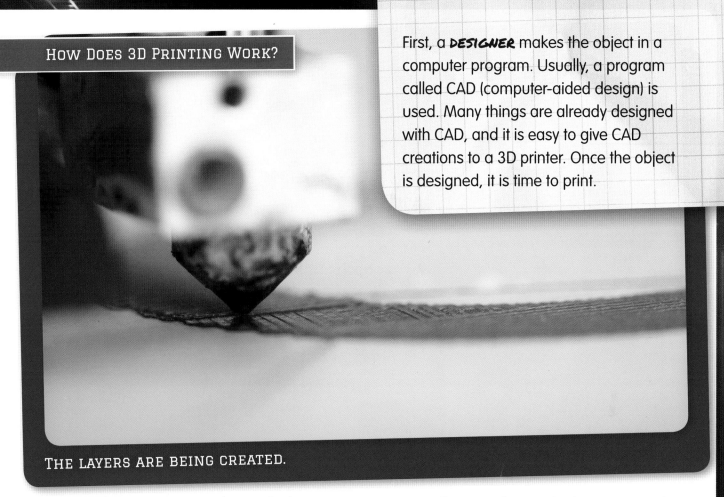

THE LAYERS ARE BEING CREATED.

First, a *DESIGNER* makes the object in a computer program. Usually, a program called CAD (computer-aided design) is used. Many things are already designed with CAD, and it is easy to give CAD creations to a 3D printer. Once the object is designed, it is time to print.

A normal printer sprays a layer of ink onto paper to create writing and pictures. The 3D printer is very similar but, instead of ink, it uses other materials. Plastic is the most common. Instead of putting one layer down, a 3D printer builds lots and lots of very thin layers one on top of the other.

Eventually a 3D object is built up, just as if you built an object out of building blocks, one layer at a time. When the object is first being printed, the material used, such as plastic, is in a powder or liquid form. The material is then fused together with lasers or glue.

A BIGGER 3D PRINTER

After all these steps are completed, a 3D object has been created! Movie studios would use big 3D printers, which can print big objects.

CAMERAS

Cameras are machines which turn light into pictures, and they are very important pieces of technology when filming a movie. Let's take a closer look at light to find out how cameras work.

CAMERA

LIGHT Light is a wave of energy that travels in a straight line. We see things because light reflects off an object and then goes into our eye. Our eyes have curved *LENSES* at the front. The lenses direct the light waves so they hit a small area at the back of our eye, called the *RETINA*. Our brain turns all the light hitting the retina into a picture that we can see.

Cameras also use a lens to direct light onto a small area. Some cameras direct light onto a piece of film, which records an image. A digital camera directs light onto a sensor, which records the image using a computer instead.

THE SENSOR OR FILM IS LIKE A RETINA.

YOUR EYE IS ACTUALLY MADE UP OF 2 MILLION DIFFERENT PARTS. DON'T WORRY, WE'RE NOT GOING TO GO THROUGH THEM ALL.

FRAME RATE

Cameras only let light hit the film or sensor when a button is pressed. Usually, there is a shutter curtain behind the lens which stops any light getting through. When the button is pressed, the shutter curtain lifts and the picture is taken. When shooting a movie, this happens again and again. The amount of times the shutter opens and closes (and therefore the amount of images you take) per second is called the frame rate.

MOVING PICTURES

Human eyes are able to see 20 images a second. If the eye sees more than 20 images a second, the images begin to blur into one. Most movies use 24 frames per second. When these frames, or images, are put together, our brain can't keep up, and the pictures merge together and look like one moving image. Some **DIRECTORS** want their movies to look even smoother, so they shoot at 48 or 60 frames per second. In the future, technology might allow movies to have even higher frame rates, which will look even smoother.

PIGEONS CAN SEE MANY MORE IMAGES PER SECOND THAN HUMANS. BECAUSE THEIR EYES ARE SO FAST, OUR MOVIES WOULD LOOK LIKE A LOT OF STILL PICTURES. A MOVIE FOR PIGEONS WOULD NEED TO HAVE AT LEAST 250 FRAMES PER SECOND.

23

FILM

Film is a type of material that is very sensitive to light. The light creates pictures on the film, which can then be used to show movies. Film was used all the time in the past. Today, digital cameras, which use computers and sensors, are usually used instead. However, there are some directors who still like to use film. Some people prefer film because they think it looks better, or because it gives a particular effect. Some people also say that using film can be cheaper for a big movie.

A REEL OF FILM

FILM GETS DAMAGED OVER TIME.

PRODUCTION
DIRECTOR
CAMERA
DATE   SC

There are some problems with film, too. Cameras that use film are bigger and more difficult to move and use. Also, if you want to watch the movie, you have to have the reels of film in your hand so you can feed into a projector.

IF A MOVIE IS AN HOUR AND A HALF LONG, IT HAS PROBABLY USED AROUND 2,470 METRES OF FILM.

FILM MEETS LIGHT

Film is made of thin plastic and covered in silver halide crystals. The crystals that are hit by light will **REACT** and change. However, you can't see this change straight away. First, the film is washed with a **CHEMICAL**. All the silver halide crystals that were not hit by light are removed. This creates the image that was captured by the camera. In movies, lots of pictures are taken every second and are joined together in a reel of film. When the film is shown at the cinema, the film is fed through a projector.

THE FILM IS DEVELOPED IN A DARK ROOM, SO THE CRYSTALS DO NOT REACT TO ANY MORE LIGHT.

THE DARK ROOM! PERFECT. NO LIGHT MEANS NO CAMERAS! NOW T—

CRASH!

OW, OW, OW! I'VE FALLEN OVER. OH THIS HURTS — THIS ROOM IS WAY WORSE THAN THE CAMERAS! I'M GETTING OUT OF HERE.

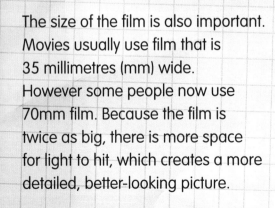

A PIECE OF 70MM FILM

The size of the film is also important. Movies usually use film that is 35 millimetres (mm) wide. However some people now use 70mm film. Because the film is twice as big, there is more space for light to hit, which creates a more detailed, better-looking picture.

DIGITAL MOVIE-MAKING

In 2002, Star Wars Episode II: Attack of the Clones was released. It was one of the first big movies to be completely digital. No film was used, and each camera used sensors and computers. Digital technology has completely changed how movies can be made.

A movie made using digital cameras looks cleaner and clearer. It doesn't get damaged over time, either. Because it is a computer file, it can also be copied and sent electronically, which means it can be watched from any computer or cinema in the world.

Digital technology also makes things smaller, easier to use and often cheaper. If you listen to digital music, you can have thousands and thousands of songs on a tiny little device. Phones, televisions and computers have all become smaller and more powerful with digital technology. The same is true for movies – digital cameras are much cheaper and more lightweight.

Easy to Carry

Digital cameras are used for things like documentaries or movies that are shot in a place that is hard to get to. By using digital technology, moviemakers do not need to carry round long reels of film, or big heavy cameras. This makes it perfect for following a lion through a **SAVANNAH**, or filming a whole movie in the jungle.

Your First Camera

Digital cameras are easier for people who have just started filming. If someone wants to make a small, simple movie, they probably won't have film, a dark room or chemicals to develop film. Digital cameras usually cost less money and are much easier to use if someone is learning how to make a movie.

NOW THAT DIGITAL CAMERAS ARE BECOMING MORE POPULAR, MORE AND MORE PEOPLE ARE MAKING THEIR OWN MOVIES.

HMMM, ALL THIS TALK OF CLEVER, DIGITAL TECHNOLOGY HAS GIVEN ME AN IDEA FOR AN INVENTION. AN INVENTION THAT MIGHT GET ME OUT OF THIS INTERVIEW... ALL I NEED IS A FIZZCRACKLE, A TIME CRYSTAL, A COUPLE OF PAPERCLIPS AND ABOUT TWO PAGES' WORTH OF TIME!

THERE IS PLENTY MORE AMAZING TECHNOLOGY TO BE MADE IN THE FUTURE! WE ARE GOING TO NEED LOTS OF BRIGHT NEW SCIENTISTS, ENGINEERS AND MATHEMATICIANS TO MAKE IT HAPPEN. HERE ARE SOME OF THE THINGS THAT THEY MIGHT BE WORKING ON...

VIRTUAL REALITY

Virtual reality, or VR, is a technology that makes you feel like you are inside a virtual, computer-created world. VR uses a special headset with a screen inside. As you look around and explore, the screen shows you all the different parts of the virtual world.

THIS CHILD IS WEARING A VIRTUAL REALITY HEADSET.

VR takes you to all sorts of strange places. You might be taken to the top of a virtual mountain, an underwater shipwreck or even to another planet. Some VR uses sensor technology to track where a person is and what direction they are walking in. This allows the person to walk around the virtual reality world too. This type of VR needs to be used in special rooms so the person doesn't bump into anything.

APPS AND PHONES

App developers and movie studios are working together to create apps to be used while watching a movie. The apps give extra information, videos and behind-the-scenes facts about the movie.

Some movies are even turning apps into part of the story, so the viewers can look on their phones to find out information that the characters in the movie don't know!

THESE TYPES OF APPS ARE OFTEN CALLED 'SECOND SCREEN APPS'.

STREAMING SITES

Instead of seeing the latest movie at a cinema, many people buy or rent them from a **STREAMING** site. These are sites which have a big selection of movies, which you can watch by streaming them over the internet. Usually, you need to pay a **SUBSCRIPTION** to the site. Nobody is sure what will happen to cinemas in the future, but streaming movies from devices such as computers and tablets is getting more popular.

IN THE FUTURE, MANY MOVIES WON'T BE SHOWN AT CINEMAS, AND WILL ONLY BE WATCHED ONLINE.

HOME TIME

BRRRRRRRIII
NNNNNGGGGG

ANOTHER DAY OF STEM SCHOOL IS OVER... WHICH MEANS THAT IT IS TIME TO SELF-DESTRUCT THE WHOLE BUILDING! AH, MUCH BETTER. THOSE CAMERAS CAN'T MAKE A MOVIE ABOUT A SCHOOL THAT DOESN'T EXIST! DID I MENTION THAT I REALLY DON'T LIKE INTERVIEWS?

OH, DON'T WORRY CHILDREN — ONCE THOSE CAMERA ROBOTS GO AWAY, I'LL SECRETLY REBUILD STEM SCHOOL ALL OVER AGAIN. MAYBE I'LL USE ONE OF THOSE 3D PRINTERS. ANYWAY, IF YOU LIKE STEM AND WANT TO LEARN MORE, THEN READ ON...

You could see if your school has any after school STEM programs. Try talking to your teacher or your parents about how to get involved in STEM. You could also try thinking like a scientist, mathematician or engineer yourself! STEM is all about solving problems — next time you see a problem, think about how it can be solved. You might be able to test your idea and see if it works. That is what STEM is all about.

FOLLOW THESE LINKS TO CARRY ON LEARNING ONLINE:

SCIENCE EXPERIMENTS
– www.funology.com/science-experiments/

BBC SCIENCE
– http://www.bbc.co.uk/education/subjects/z6svr82

BBC MATHS
– http://www.bbc.co.uk/education/subjects/zjxhfg8

CRASHCOURSE SCIENCE VIDEOS
– www.youtube.com/user/crashcoursekids

GLOSSARY

ACTORS	people who performs on stage, in films or on television programs
ANIMATED	lots of images, drawn by hand or computer, which create a moving image when put together
CGI	Computer Generated Imagery: images and special effects created by computers for TV and film
CHEMICAL	a substance that is usually produced artificially by scientists
DESIGNER	a person who plans how something will look or work before it is made
DIRECTORS	people who control how a film is made and manage the actors and crew
EDITING	changing or correcting a piece of work
FILM INDUSTRY	economic activity involved with the production and release of films
FILMING	recording a movie
HOLLYWOOD	the United States of America's film industry, based in California
IMAGE	a picture or graphic
LENSES	curved pieces of glass that can direct or disperse light
MECHANICAL	operated by a machine
PADDLES	poles with broad, flat blades at the end
PROJECTOR	a device which shines light onto a wall or screen, usually used to show a film or some pictures
PROTOTYPE	the first working version of a device or product, which all other forms are copied from
REACT	(in science) when a substance chemically or physically changes in response to stimuli
RETINA	the area at the back of the eye which senses light and sends information to the brain
ROTATING	turning around a central point or axis
ROTORS	parts of a machine that spin around, e.g., the blades of a helicopter which spin to create flight
SAVANNAH	a grassy area of land with few trees, found in hot countries such as those in Africa
SCENES	parts of a film or TV programme where things happen in the same place
SHOTS	uninterrupted moving images in a film or TV programme, created when the camera starts filming to when it stops
STREAMING	listening to music or watching a video directly from the internet
SUBSCRIPTION	continuously getting a product or service by sending regular payments
SYSTEMS	sets of things that work together to do specific jobs
TISSUE	groups of cells that are similar to each other and do the same job

INDEX

PHOTO CREDITS

Front Cover – ixer, Stephen Mcsweeny, Jag_cz, Alex Staroseltsev, MIGUEL GARCIA SAAVEDRA, Richard Peterson, Bosko. 2 – ixer, Stephen Mcsweeny, Jag_cz, Alex Staroseltsev, MIGUEL GARCIA SAAVEDRA, Richard Peterson, Bosko 4 – pixome, Lorena Fernandez. 5 – science photo. 6 – Thomas Wolf, Filip Fuxa, Eadweard Muybridge, Victorgrigas. 7 – Gorodenkoff, Liu zishan. 8 – François Chauveau, Marco Becerra, Eunostos, Tomacco. 9 – By similis, Studio 72. 10 – Cmglee, Ekaterina Kebal. 11 – Richard Bartz, Franciscoceba, Hadrian. 12 – LI CHAOSHU, Alena Ohneva, Prosto Vov4i, Carodejnice, Swasdee, Quarta. 13 – SUNG YOON JO. 14 – Who is Danny, oliveromg. 15 – Rubendene, Sean Devine, Ulvi Yagubov, SilviaC. 16 – iNK Stories, Mounirzok, Motones. 17 – Thomas 89, zack snyder flickr, William Tung. 18 – plantic, Marnikus, SilviaC, IQRemix, Wikicommons. 19 – Montri Nipitvittaya, Love Silhouette, LALS STOCK. 20 – Panda Vector, Ninchik, Sparkus design, lady-luck, olegator, FabrikaSimf. 21 – nikkytok, Gui le chat. 22 – lapandr, udaix. 23 – Wikicommons, gladcov. 24 – Witold Andrzejewski, Serge Ka. 25 – Volkova Vera, Uncle Ulee, Zigmej. 26 – ycanada_news, AAAndrey A. 27 – Alta Oosthuizen, zlikovec. 28 – wavebreakmedia. 29 – Billion Photos, Tero Vesalainen. 30 – Rawpixel.com. Border on all pages: Bosko. Graph Paper – The_Pixel. Tess Tube – mayrum.
Images are courtesy of Shutterstock.com. With thanks to Getty Images, Thinkstock Photo and iStockphoto.

25 Aug 2022.

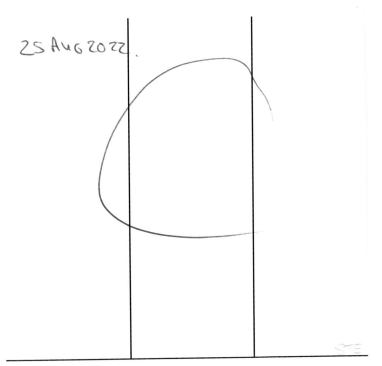

Please renew or return items by the date
shown on your receipt

www.hertfordshire.gov.uk/libraries

Renewals and enquiries: 0300 123 4049

Textphone for hearing or 0300 123 4041
speech impaired users:

32 11.16

527 554 79 X